Termites

by Mary Bach

illustrated by
Tammie Speer-Lyon

 Richard C. Owen Publishers, Inc.
Katonah, New York

TO LOCKERS

My name is Kate.
I love to skate.

I'm a Termite.
Termites are
beginning hockey players.

When Termites skate we wear:
sweat shirts, sweat pants,
thick socks, gloves, helmets,

knee pads, elbow pads, and hockey skates.

Our coaches are nice.
They help us a lot.

They show us how to hold
our hockey sticks.

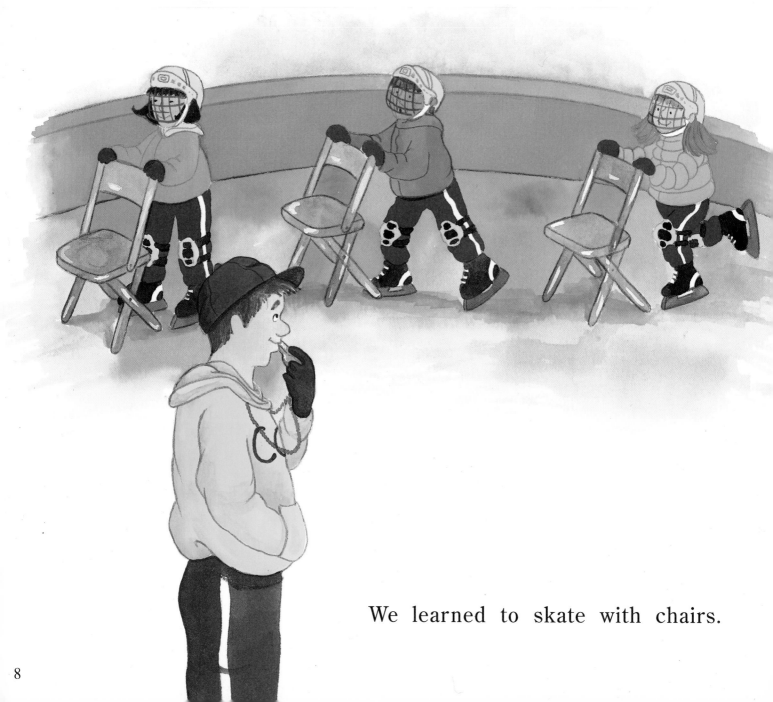

We learned to skate with chairs.

When we stopped using chairs,
we fell down a lot.

Now we don't fall down as much – just sometimes.

Our coaches make everything fun.
They play "Cat and Mouse" and "Tag" with us.
Coach is always "it."
We learn to skate fast, turn, and stop.

At first, for stopping we used the wall.
Now we don't.

We practice shooting goals.

After practice we drink lots of water.
We need it!

Soon we will play
our first hockey game.

It's great being a Termite!